Are You a Cliff Dweller?

by Ms. Hogan's class
with Tony Stead

capstone

Cliff Dwellers

Are you a cliff dweller? Cliff dwellers are people who made their homes in cliffs.

Their lives were very different. Their homes were made from rock. Today, many homes are made from wood, stone, or brick. Read on to find out about different homes.

Long ago a group of Native Americans made their homes in this cliff.

Houses

Houses are important because they protect people from danger and bad weather.

People live in different kinds of homes. Homes can look different. They can be different sizes. Often homes are built from materials that are available.

Tepees

Long ago, Native Americans in the Great Plains lived in tepees. Tepees, which are cone shaped, were made from animal skins and wooden poles.

They were durable and could be put up and taken down quickly. They kept Native Americans snug and warm in winter and cool in the summer.

Caves

People lived in caves that were already formed by nature. Caves were dark, cold, and damp.

Cave people drew plain and simple pictures of animals, people, and designs on cave walls. These drawings told a story.

Igloos

The Eskimos are people who live in the Arctic. They made shelters from snow and ice called igloos.

Igloos can only be found in cold places.

Igloos

Houseboats

Some houses can move! People can live on a houseboat, which is a house and a boat combined.

If you would like to move from place to place, a houseboat might be the kind of home for you.

Apartments

Apartment buildings have lots of people. They often have elevators, staircases, and balconies. Some even have pools!

Each apartment has its own number.

Just like homes from long ago, homes today protect us and give us shelter. They are also places where we live as a family.

by Alexander, Emerson, Emma, Gabriella, Hana, Hero, Jack, Jayden, Joshuah, Isabelle, Kaiden, Leah, Mariam, Makenzie, Neel, Nyerah, Reegan, Violet, Yaser